"Emergency Pizza Ordering 911"

Ordering Pizza Without Annoying Us

TRICIA WOOD

Copyright © 2024
Tricia Wood

All rights are reserved. No part of this book may be reproduced, distributed, or transmitted in any form or by any means, including photocopying, recording, or other electronic or mechanical methods, without the prior written permission of the author, except in the case of brief quotations embodied in critical reviews and certain other noncommercial uses permitted by copyright law.

Dedication

To all the unsung heroes of the food service world—this one's for you. To my incredible co-workers and bosses at Papa's Pizza, thank you for becoming more than just colleagues—you've become my family. We share a bond that only those who've braved the chaos of the kitchen and the craziness of the dining room can truly understand. Your joy, support, and camaraderie make it all worthwhile.

I love you all, and I wouldn't trade our shared shenanigans for anything.

Contents

Dedication iii

Introduction v

Chapter One: The Subtle Art Of Ordering A Pizza 1

Chapter Two: The Do's And DON'Ts Of Ordering Pizza- Thou Shalt Not Mess With The Margherita 8

Chapter Three: The Sandwich Chronicles: The Case Of The Eccentric Orders And The Side Dish Shenanigans 19

Chapter Four: The Order And Delivery Situations: Where We Dive Deep Into Frustration, Your Etiquette Takes A Vacation, And The Cheese Invades Our Patience 29

Chapter Five: The Great Customer Showdown: Complaining Your Way Out Of A Good Meal 36

Chapter Six: The Art Of Free Food Schemes, Timed Orders, And The Sauce Saga .. 44

Chapter Seven: Eggplants, Egos, And Eccentricities 51

Chapter Eight: The Last Slice: How To Order Like A Pro And Keep Everyone Happy 60

    Right Way: 61

    Wrong Way: 62

    Right Way: 64

    Wrong Way: 65

    Right Way: 66

    Wrong Way: 67

Introduction

This is my first attempt at writing a book, and I must admit, it began as a therapeutic outlet to vent out after a particularly chaotic day at work. My journey with Papa's Pizza spans over 20 years, with breaks here and there, and I have Chuck Green and Ken Ford to thank for this wild ride. I've dabbled in various careers—each with its unique challenges and rewards. I was a lead teacher at a daycare until a severe back injury forced me to change paths. I tried my hand at computer support, but the monotony and immobility of cubicle life were not for me. Running a kitchen in a bustling bar was thrilling, but that chapter closed when the bar was sold.

Through all these experiences, I discovered a profound truth: my heart belongs to Papa's Pizza. There's something incredibly special about this place. It's exciting, crazy, frustrating, stressful, and absolutely wonderful all at once! The unpredictable nature of each day fuels my passion. No two days are the same, and that keeps me on my toes. Every shift brings new challenges and surprises, making the job anything but mundane.

Everything in this book stems from my personal experiences at Papa's. While some anecdotes might be unique to our establishment, I believe many can resonate with those familiar with the pizza industry. From the kind-hearted customers to the quirky ones, every interaction has shaped this book. Whether you're a pizza aficionado, a fellow employee, or just someone looking for a good laugh, I hope you find these stories as entertaining and enlightening as they were for me.

A heartfelt thank you to all our customers—both wonderful and not-so-wonderful. Your kindness and quirks have provided endless inspiration. And to Chuck Green and Ken Ford, thank you for the opportunity to be part of Papa's Pizza. This might end up being a truly short book, but it's packed with tales of laughter, lessons, and life from behind the counter.

So, let's begin this journey through the highs and lows, the hilarity and chaos, and the sheer unpredictability that makes working at Papa's Pizza an adventure worth sharing.

Chapter One:
The Subtle Art Of Ordering A Pizza

Craving a slice of mouth-watering pizza that will transport you to the sun-drenched streets of Naples, Italy? But feeling intimidated by the process of ordering, don't worry, dear pizza fanatic. We've got your back, and we're here to guide you through it all. No pun is intended! But honestly, who are you and what have you done to your humane self? How, in a world filled with modern technology, can you not know something as basic as ordering a pizza? Okay, fine, we totally get it. Don't worry; we'll ignore this shocking information for now and move on.

Our pizza shop is a delicious heaven for all pizza lovers, and every bite is a journey to flavor nirvana. And here's a little secret: we're proudly old school. Forget emails or faxes; that's just not our style. We take orders through pigeons, canaries, and sometimes ravens... Oops, gotcha, just kidding! You can call us through your trusty landline or mobile phone.

But if you really want to get the full sensory experience, come on in and order in person. The aroma of our freshly baked crust, the sizzle of our savory toppings, and the warmth of our cozy atmosphere will give you an experience that simply can't be replicated through a screen.

Walking into our pizzaiolo, you will be greeted by the rich, enticing smells of dough and cheese mingling in the air. It's like stepping into a warm, cheesy ocean. Dive into those cheesy waves and let your worries melt away.

Now, let's talk about the heart and soul of our pizzeria—our quirky and lovable characters. From the charismatic owner who hand-tosses each crust with love to the quirky delivery guy who always has a cheesy joke up his sleeve, we're a diverse and dynamic bunch.

So, if you are extremely eager to meet our characters who run this pizzeria and are our backstage, behind-the-scene heroes, you can meet them now through your wonderful imagination skills just imagine the master pizzaiolo, his hands a blur as he expertly twirls the dough in the air, all while sharing tales of his Nonna's secret tomato sauce recipe. He'll wink at you and say, "A pizza without love is like a car without wheels. It ain't going nowhere!" and let's not forget our delivery guy, who has a knack for showing up at your door with a smile and a joke saying "Ladies, I have brought mushroom to the party. Because it seems like you were searching for some fungi!" This guy is hilarious and always there to brighten your day with his witty and quirky jokes. He's like a diamond in the rough at our pizza place, loving his work and making every delivery special.

Now, if their not-so-funny jokes haven't already killed you from laughter, let me show you how to cross this red sea of ketchup and marinara. This girl loathes tomato sauce and ketchup, it dishonors the pizza gods.

For starters, let's begin with the Walk-Ins. Now, first things first: if you're coming into order in person, be prepared for a little human interaction. Isn't that Shocking, right? Our cashier will greet you with a friendly "Hi, how are you today?" At this point, you'll need to let us know if the order is for here or to go. Please, for the love of pizza and everything holy, respond to this question before diving into your order. We can't proceed until we hit "dine in" or "to go" on the screen.

Got a split bill situation? Let us know upfront. It's bad enough you're that cheap and can't do the math, but we can't have anyone paying a penny more than they owe because all hell will break loose and it's a pain in the ass to split the bill after we've put the order through, so spare us the hassle.

Oh, and another thing: put your phone down when you come in to order. It's extremely rude to be talking on the phone while placing or picking up an order. You're basically saying you're more important than us and that you don't have to pay attention to us like we're beneath you. Guess what? We're not! And you aren't royalty and even If you were, it's just bad manners and highly snobbish of you. I personally won't help a customer if they're on the phone. I will ignore you until you hang up or put them on hold. Respect goes both ways, folks.

3

Not ready to order? Don't stand at the counter. Step to the side while you look at the menu. There are usually other customers behind you, and we won't make them wait while you decide what you want to eat. It has happened several times that I've had to go around the counter to help the next customer because someone wouldn't move aside while they were still looking at the menu, and might I add, it was extremely annoying. So, I helped everyone else until she was the last customer in the store, and then I helped her. If you're going to be rude to others, I will be rude to you. It's as simple as that. Most of our customers are respectful, but there are always a few who just don't get it. I just don't know what is wrong with these people; they are hopeless.

Now, for those who call ahead to place their orders. Calling ahead is awesome. I love that. I'd even like to bow down and curtsy for your oh-so-gentle consideration. But let's get a few things straight to make this as smooth as possible.

When you call, our cashier will answer with the name of the store followed by "Is this for pick-up or delivery?" Please do not start placing your order before you answer this question. We cannot go any further until we hit one of those two options on our screen. Also, it's rude to start barking orders without greeting us first, mind your manners.

If you are ordering for pick-up, the cashier will read your name back to you. Don't be shocked or surprised by this. We assure you we are not interested in you or obsessed with you like some creepy stalker; we are just living in the 21st century and have this magical thing called caller ID. Now, if it's for delivery, the cashier will read your address. Again, it's just modern technology at work. If we ask for your address, it means you haven't ordered from us before and we need to ensure you're within our delivery range. So, please, know where you are. Saying you're babysitting or at a friend's house won't help us get the food to you. We need an actual address. Check a piece of mail or ask whose house it is before you call. Trust me, it'll save us both a lot of time and hassle and you'll get your pizza faster!

Lastly, the pièce de résistance, aka the most important part, is to make sure you know what you want to order before you call. We don't have time to sit on hold while you run around asking everyone what they want. Trust me, it's not music to our ears hearing you shout, "Who wants extra cheese?" or "Does anyone want pepperoni?" And we definitely don't need to know how many people hate pineapple on their pizza. Seriously, get your crew's orders sorted out beforehand, even if it means writing it down. You can even use the talk-to-text feature on your phone if you're feeling particularly lazy.

And please, for the sake of all that is cheesy and delicious, don't have two people on the phone at the same time. First, it's impossible to hear either one of you clearly. Second, you inevitably end up talking over each other, turning a simple order into a confusing, chaotic mess. Save us—and yourself—the headache.

It may seem obvious, but seriously, don't call us while you're at the car wash. Guess what? When you do these things, we can't hear you! We're pizza pros, not noise-canceling experts. And please, don't call from your car with the window down—unless you want us to hear every honk and breeze.

And here's a whopper: please, please, do not, I repeat, do not call us from the bathroom. We really don't need to hear your toilet flushing in the background while we're trying to take your order. Trust me, that's just not cool on so many levels! Let's keep our pizza chat flush with good vibes, not from bathroom acoustics, okay?

Also, please spare us a hundred questions about what we serve. We're here to make pizza, not give you a detailed verbal menu tour, and we don't have time to read the whole menu to you. And let me tell you something truly wild: there's this thing called the Internet. It has this nifty feature called the World Wide Web, where you can check out our menu in your free time. I know, it is completely shocking that something like that exists, right?

Another crucial point that I want to add is that it is extremely baffling, yet it happens a lot. So, seriously people don't call us back to add more to your order. That just drags out the process and will make your order take longer. Who needs that? By the way, how does someone slip from your mind entirely and how can you forget a whole person like big uncle Willie? Were you trying to order before he walked through the door, or did you just not notice him sitting on the couch out there? I get it if you forgot a side of cheese or dressing, but believe it or not, some folks call back to add a whole pizza or sandwich. Hence, if you absolutely must add on, do it pronto—not 20 minutes later when your other food's already hitting the table. Let's keep it smooth and simple, okay?

Just embrace the Old School, folks. We're a pizza shop that enjoys the calm pace of tradition in an age of AI and digital everything. Please resist the urge to email or fax us your order. We thrive on the personal touch—call or swing by to place your order. We promise it'll be worth it.

So, step on in or give us a ring. Let us whisk your taste buds away and stir up those emotions with our tantalizing slices. Because here, it's not just about the food—it's about the whole experience. Trust us, and you'll savor every moment you are here.

Chapter Two:
The Do's And DON"Ts Of Ordering Pizza-
Thou Shalt Not Mess With The Margherita

So, you think ordering a pizza is as simple as picking up the phone and saying, "One large pepperoni, please"? Oh, how adorably naïve you are child, may god bless your heart! There's an entire protocol to this process, and if you don't follow it, well, you're just asking for a culinary catastrophe.

In the grand world of pizza, there are sacred rules that keep the universe of cheese and toppings in harmony. One of the most revered principles? The Pizza is sacred, and thou shalt not mess with it.

Let's take the classic Margherita pizza for example—simple and elegant, with its divine trio of tomatoes, mozzarella, and a hint of basil. This is not a canvas for your culinary experiments. If you dare to alter or butcher it, prepare for the Italian ancestors and pizza gods to unleash a collective curse from the heavens above. It's the pizza equivalent of the Mona Lisa; a timeless masterpiece that should be left untouched. Adding extra toppings or requesting bizarre modifications is like slapping a mustache on Da Vinci's finest work—an abomination of epic proportions.

In essence, if you order a Pizza, respect its traditional simplicity. Don't ask for a mountain of toppings or request it be "lightly well done." Just let it be.

Also, let's clear up a misconception: dinner may be on our menu, but we absolutely despise making them. Too many moving parts. Salad, garlic bread, boiling water—it's like juggling flaming swords while riding a unicycle. Who has the time for all of this?

Now, onto the main event and the crux of our conversation: the sacred order of ordering pizza. At our place, it goes like this: pizzas, sandwiches, salads, sides, and drinks—in that exact sequence. This isn't just some illogical list; there's a method to the madness. The goal is to make sure everything arrives at your doorstep; hot and ready, not lukewarm and sad.

We know at a sit-down restaurant; they bring you appetizers to munch on while you wait for your main course. And that truly sounds delightful, right? Well, we tried that, but then your appetizers sat there, getting cold, staring at you with a forlorn look as you waited for your pizza to finish its journey through the fiery furnace. Not a good look.

So, we flipped the script. Here, we start with the item that takes the longest to cook (hint: that's the pizza). While that's doing its thing, we whip up the smaller, quicker items. It's a fine-tuned ballet of dough, cheese, and toppings, all working together in perfect harmony to land on your table simultaneously. Yes, it's the complete opposite of what you'd expect, but hey, welcome to our world of Mozzarella, and Marinara, don't worry, we also serve other crazy combos as well.

And let's talk about those sides. Garlic bread and salads are like the supporting actors of the pizza's central character. They're crucial, sure, but they don't demand the same spotlight. Sides are the Robin to pizza's Batman, the Chewbacca to pizza's Han Solo. Essential, but let's be real, you're here for the main attraction.

Drinks? They're the unsung silent heroes, quietly waiting in the wings to quench your thirst after a glorious bite of that cheesy goodness. We save them for last because, well, they don't need an oven or a grill. They just need a glass and a little bit of love.

In conclusion, ordering from us is like following a complex recipe for success. Ignore the steps at your risk. Get it right, and you'll have a harmonious meal where everything is at its peak. Get it wrong, and you'll end up with a cold appetizer, a lukewarm pizza, and the bitter taste of regret.

Next, let's dive into the nitty-gritty of how to and how NOT to order each type of item. Starting with pizza.

Ordering a half or whole topping? No problem that's perfectly acceptable and totally fine. But when you start ordering four different types of quarter toppings, things get a bit... annoying.

And then there is the real kicker: "The ultimate and glorious everything" pizza. Do you not realize we have over 19 toppings? That's $38 extra on top of the cost of the pizza! Not only is it a wallet-buster, but it's nearly impossible to cook right, and you'll probably end up complaining. Yet, here I am, a fake smile plastered on, pretending like it's a totally reasonable request. So PLEASE, for the love of all the holy cheese gods, do not ask for an everything pizza. It's a monstrosity that no oven should ever have to suffer through.

Also, stop with the "lightly well done" nonsense. That just means cooked. Stop with the "little extra sauce or cheese" gimmick. You're trying to be cheap and not pay for the extra. Guess what? We charge you for it, even if it's only a little extra.

When asking for well-done or lightly cooked, understand we go by our perception, not yours. So it might not be exactly the way you want it. Suck it up; it's a pizza, not a $50 steak. I understand you're spending your hard-earned money, but when you change the way of seeing how we do things; it won't always be perfect.

Please, do NOT ask for toppings on the left or right side of the pizza. I'm not even going to explain why. Just think about it. One hint: the pizza is round.

So there you have it—the dos and don'ts of ordering pizza. Follow these guidelines, and you'll make everyone's life a little easier, including your own.

But what if the protagonist; good old Lexi, a new employee at the pizza place, is a perfectionist who prides themselves on always making the perfect pizza? They've been trained to follow the customer's requests and ensure each pizza is made exactly to their liking. However, the antagonist, intimidating Marco the boss of the pizza place, is a strict and grumpy owner who has been in the business for years and believes in doing things his way—no exceptions.

One day, a customer named Peter comes in and asks for a pizza with all of the toppings on one half and no toppings on the other half. Lexi, following her training, starts to make the pizza exactly as the customer requested. But Marco walks by and sees what she is doing.

"What are you doing?" Marco snarls, looking over the Lexi's shoulder.

"I'm making the pizza the customer asked for," Lexi responds confidently.

"But that's not how we do things here. We cannot put that many toppings on the whole pizza, let alone half a pizza. It won't cook right, and the customer will complain and want their money back."

Lexi starts to feel conflicted. She knows she is supposed to follow the customer's requests, but she also wants to follow her boss's orders.

"I'm sorry, I'll fix it," Lexi says, trying to please both Peter and Marco.

However, Peter sees the interaction and starts to get angry. "I asked you to make the pizza in this way for a reason. Can't you just do what I'm paying you to do?" he snaps at Lexi.

Now, Lexi is torn between wanting to please the customer and wanting to follow her boss's orders. She knows that if she doesn't do things her boss's way, she could lose her job. But she also doesn't want to disappoint the customer or make a bad pizza.

In the end, Lexi gives in to Peter's demands and makes the pizza exactly how he wants it. But when he takes a bite, he complains that it's not cooked enough. Now, Lexi feels defeated and regrets not standing up to the customer and following their boss's instructions.

The moral of the Story: The customer is NOT always right! And I will say that again and again—the customer is NOT always right!!!

As a dedicated pizza maker, I live by a strict code when it comes to assembling and cooking our delicious creations. Perfection is my middle name, and I've been known to give my co-workers a piece of my mind when they get sloppy. But lately, my love for pizza perfection is being put to the test by some truly ridiculous customer requests.

Emergency Pizza Ordering 911

With customers ordering half-topping pizzas, which is no problem, I can handle that. But then, they go and ask for quarter toppings—four different kinds, no less! It's like they wake up in the morning thinking, "How can I make my pizza maker's life a living nightmare today?" And don't even get me started on the person who asked for thirds. We do not, I repeat, do NOT accommodate thirds. The pie is cut into eight slices, folks. We could cut it into six slices (still annoying but doable). But cutting it into eight slices divided into thirds? That's mathematically impossible (I think). Yes, that's what she wanted. Seriously, people I need to have a serious conversation with your calculus and math teacher.

Then there are the cheapskates who ask for a "little extra sauce" or a "little extra cheese." Spoiler alert: we still charge you for the extra, even if it's just a smidgen, a dash, or even a sprinkle. And let me tell you, Buddy, I know who you are. I've got my eyes on you, Marcus, you sly moron. I know exactly what you're trying to pull here—I've seen plenty like you. You can't escape my laser-focused gaze and razor-sharp wit. I will make sure you pay for every single thing you order, down to the last crumb.

Now, let's talk about the folks who want their pizza "lightly well done." What does that even mean? Did I mishear the order, or are you confusing us with a steakhouse? Snap out of your daze! If you're serious, please, enlighten me: what on earth is "lightly well done" in the binary world of cooked or not cooked, folks? Are you trying to school us on pizza perfection, or are you just another fake Italian who thinks they know more than our Master Pizzaiolo Antonio? This guy has been making pizzas since before you were born. So, drop the know-it-all attitude, kiddo. We don't cater to narcissists and toxic people here.

However, the crown jewel of absurdity doesn't end here it truly shines, when you ask for toppings on the left or right side of the pizza. I literally have no words for these customers—they've elevated madness to an art form. Tell me, folks, did Euclid, the father of geometry, rewrite the rules overnight, or are you channeling some ancient ghost who still believes the earth is flat? The pizza is round, people! It has no sides. How exactly am I supposed to put toppings on just one side of it? It's like asking a painter to color only the left half of a circle. Pure genius

You guys have no idea, but because of you, my work life has become a never-ending battle between my desire to please my customers and my need to maintain order and sanity in the kitchen as if things weren't already chaotic enough at home.

But every time, I end up feeling like a colossal failure, no matter how hard I try. Maybe it's time to think about a career change—perhaps to something blissfully free of picky, demanding customers who have zero appreciation for the unique and honorable art of pizza making.

Chapter Three:
The Sandwich Chronicles: The Case Of The Eccentric Orders And The Side Dish Shenanigans

Let's face it, we all agree and know that the side dishes are just there to keep the main event from feeling lonely. I mean, you ever notice how the salad always seems like it's just tagging along, hoping to catch some of the glory from the sandwich that's clearly hogging all the attention?

In the heart of our busy pizza shop, where the scent of sizzling meats and melting cheese is as constant as the hum of the espresso machine, I stand as the grand conductor of this culinary symphony. The kitchen is a whirlwind of activity—orders flying in, ingredients flying out, and me, the humble maestro, orchestrating it all with a mix of frustration and flair.

Let me paint you a picture of the sandwich madness I endure daily. Picture this: it's another day in paradise, and by paradise, I mean the chaos of our kitchen. I'm elbow-deep in a sea of sandwiches and the occasional existential crisis, trying to piece together the puzzling requests that come my way. Ah, yes, the Parmesan sandwich—one of our most popular items. You'd think it's just bread, cheese, and some meat, but no, people have managed to turn it into a culinary free-for-all.

I vividly remember the time someone asked for a Parmesan sandwich with both mayo and ketchup. "Sure," I thought, "because nothing screams gourmet like combining condiments that are as different as night and day." I mean, really, who knew that a Parmesan sandwich needed to taste like a messy backyard barbecue? I did my best to smile as I prepared it, silently lamenting the fact that I couldn't slap a warning label on the sandwich that read, "Eating this may cause existential dread."

Then there's the case of the steak sandwich. We've had more requests for "extra" this and "more" that than I can count. One customer wanted a double steak with every topping available, and I'm talking about a sandwich that could double as a heart attack on a plate. "Here you go," I said, handing over a sandwich that looked like it could be used as a doorstop. "Hope you enjoy your culinary Everest."

But oh, it doesn't stop there. One day, a customer decided that a half-steak sandwich with lettuce, tomato, onion, salt, pepper, and oregano on one side and the other half with just ketchup was a great idea. "You know," I quipped to my co-worker, "I've always wanted to test my skills at culinary schizophrenia. Thanks for making that dream come true." As if half of the sandwich wasn't enough of a challenge, they wanted it "separated" into two plates to save a dollar on fries. "Ah yes," I mused, "because saving a buck is worth making our lives a complete circus."

The lunch specials are a breed of their own. One particular gem involved a customer ordering a whole cheese steak special but wanted it split onto two separate plates "just to avoid paying for fries." I mean, who needs fries when you have a sandwich that's already a meal for three? "Oh, absolutely," I said, "because the universe will somehow reward you for your penny-pinching with a sandwich that's two-thirds of the size of the regular special."

Let's not forget the burger orders. "Just give me a burger well-done," some people say as if they're not asking for a hockey puck instead of a juicy patty. "Sure," I'd reply, trying to keep the sarcasm out of my voice. "Would you like that with a side of dental work?"

Then there's the wrap section, where people seem to think that the laws of physics don't apply. "Sure, I can pack every conceivable topping into a wrap until it resembles a stuffed animal rather than food," I'd say, attempting to fold it with the grace of a magician while secretly cursing the customer's name.

Salads, now there's a category that's supposed to be simple, but somehow, every antipasto salad order turns into a scavenger hunt. "Let's see," I'd say, "Today, we're missing olives, and someone wants to double the pepperoni. Ah, the thrill of trying to remember what exactly is supposed to be on this salad. It's like a culinary game of charades."

Talking about the sideshow, which is a cook's tale of fries, cheese, and culinary catastrophe. Ah, sides. The unsung heroes of the menu. They might not be the star of the show, but they sure get their fair share of attention—mostly from people who like to turn a simple potato into a gastronomic nightmare. As the cook, I pour my heart and soul into every dish, or at least I try to. But when it comes to sides, well, it's a whole different story. Buckle up; it's about to get messy.

So, let's talk about sides. French fries, onion rings, mozzarella sticks—you know, the usual suspects. I'm not even touching wings right now because, frankly, they deserve their own soap opera. No, today's drama is all about those lovely accompaniments that should be simple but somehow manage to become culinary battlegrounds.

Take French fries. They're crispy, golden, and perfect. Well, they are until you get your hands on them. You see, there's this wild notion that adding cheese, ketchup, salt, and pepper while they're in a container for delivery is a good idea. Spoiler alert: it's not. What you're really asking for is a soggy mess of potato slop. It's like asking for a gourmet burger and then setting it on fire. But hey, the customer is always right, right? So I dutifully add your toppings, knowing full well that I'm just setting myself up for a symphony of complaints. And when you call back to gripe about your sad, limp fries, all I can think is, "I told you so." But, of course, I'd never say that. I'm too busy suppressing my inner chef, who's screaming in frustration.

Now, mozzarella sticks. Oh, mozzarella sticks, how you test my culinary soul. Some things in life are simply not meant to be, like trying to make mozzarella sticks well done. If you want them well done, you'll end up with a cheesy explosion that resembles a science experiment gone horribly wrong, or they will definitely end up resembling small, burnt logs. "Fantastic," I'd think, "another round of 'Guess the Object' from the fryer. Will it be a stick or a piece of charcoal?" And don't even get me started on cheese options. Cheddar is our only cheese-on-the-side option. That's right, no melted American, Provolone, or Mozzarella. We're not running a cheese emporium here. It's either slice it or keep dreaming. But, of course, I'm still the one left to hand over your disappointed faces.

And then there's the pièce de résistance: outrageous requests. Picture this: loaded fries with pineapple and pepperoni. That's right, pineapple and pepperoni. It's like you're trying to start a new culinary trend called "heart attack on a plate." But hey, who am I to judge? I'm just here to comply with your taste bud rebellion. And if that wasn't enough, someone else orders steak, American cheese, and bacon on fries. Are you trying to cause a nationwide cholesterol emergency? I can't, in good conscience, serve such a monstrosity, but denying a paying customer is a whole different level of moral dilemma.

Now, substitutions. Let's talk about them. Ranch or hot sauce for marinara? Easy peasy. But when you start asking for melted American cheese or mozzarella sticks, I have to put on my best "I'm totally not annoyed" face. "No, we don't have melted American cheese," I'll say, biting my tongue to stop from adding, "but we do have a healthy dose of reality." And then I hand over your subpar mozzarella sticks, all while trying to maintain the integrity of our menu and my sanity.

In the end, the customer is always the king or queen of the culinary realm, and I'm just the humble cook at their mercy. I battle daily with the desire to please everyone while keeping my menu from turning into a circus act. So here's to the sides: may they always be simple, and may I always manage to keep my wits about me, even when faced with a pineapple-pepperoni disaster. Cheers to navigating this delicious chaos, one soggy fry and cheese explosion at a time!

Now let's move on to the crispy conundrum, Ah, the wings. Just the mention of them sends us into a tizzy, doesn't it? Who knew that such a simple little piece of poultry could stir up so much drama? I mean, it's just chicken with sauce on it, right? But no, when it comes to wings, we're basically running a culinary soap opera.

So, let's break this down. We sell wings by the six-pack because, apparently, six is the magic number. You want more? Sure, have twelve, eighteen, twenty-four—whatever tickles your fancy. But here's where it gets juicy: we have a smorgasbord of sauces. Mix two sauces together. Oh, absolutely—if you're ordering a bucket. If you're just getting six wings, you get one sauce. And no, we're not doing the wing dance with three wings. We're not here to waste time mixing sauces on just six wings. If you're desperate for a flavor duel, cough up for twelve.

Now, let's talk containers. Each one costs us money, so when you order six wings, don't expect us to use two containers for two sauces. That's like asking your waiter to bring out a separate plate for each crouton. Not cost-effective and, frankly, a bit too much for our taste.

Extra crispy wings? Sure, we can do that. But once we slather them in sauce and pack them up, they're going to lose their crunch faster than you can say, "Oh, no, I wanted them crispy!" The secret to keeping them semi-crispy? Sauce on the side. It's not magic; it's just common sense.

Oh, and let's address the difference between "crispy" and "well-done." "Crispy" means a delightful crunch, while "well-done" means the chicken's basically got the texture of rubber. Extra well-done? You're asking us to turn your wings into a desiccated mess. So when you demand them well done on a Friday night, it's like asking a magician to pull a rabbit out of a hat—only the rabbit's already been cooked and overcooked.

Here's the reality: on a Friday night, we're juggling about 250 to 300 orders. That's right, we're a wing-making assembly line. We don't have time to cater to every eccentric whim. If you're holding out for that extra crispy, sauce-on-the-side, well-done wing experience, try asking on a Monday. We might have the patience for it, and besides, it gives us time to recharge our will to live.

Now, picture this: I'm the overworked, slightly frazzled cook in the middle of this chaotic wing whirlwind. As the orders pile up, I'm torn between upholding my culinary ideals and just getting through the night without collapsing. It's like trying to do brain surgery while riding a unicycle.

I try to balance quality with customer demands, but inevitably, I end up making choices I'd rather not. Do I give in to the demand for extra sauce, or do I stick to my principles and risk disgruntling yet another customer? Spoiler alert: I usually choose to appease the customer. My inner foodie cries out, but my survival instincts take over.

The night's chaos reaches its peak when, in a moment of exhaustion and confusion, I mix up orders. The angry customer who's received the wrong wings doesn't exactly appreciate my artistic license. My regret and guilt weigh heavily as I face their ire. It's like having a bad breakup with a customer who's not interested in my excuses.

By the end of the night, I've survived, but not without a hefty dose of self-recrimination. My wings aren't perfect; they're not even close. But I've learned a hard truth: this job isn't just about cooking wings. It's about navigating a minefield of customer expectations and regulations. I've sacrificed a bit of my culinary pride, but I've also learned to manage my conflicts and make the best of a messy situation.

So here I am, battered but wiser, reflecting on the price of keeping my job and my sanity. My wings might not always hit the mark, but I've grown, and that's worth something—even if it means enduring the weekly wing fiasco.

And yet, amidst the chaos and comedy of culinary requests, there's a twisted joy in it all. Each day is an unpredictable adventure, where the only certainty is that nothing will go as planned. I'm just a cook, after all, navigating the absurd and hilarious world of sandwiches, one quirky order at a time. So here's to the Parmesan sandwiches with mayo and ketchup, the double steak monstrosities, and the wraps that defy the laws of physics.

In the grand scheme of things, it's all part of the fun. And as I serve up yet another sandwich with a side of sarcasm and a dash of humor, I can't help but laugh. After all, if you can't find the humor in a world where someone orders a half-steak sandwich with half ketchup and half lettuce, what can you find it in?

Moving on to the liquid chaos let me tell you how we survive a soda apocalypse without losing our minds. Let's talk drinks—because who doesn't love a good sip of irony? On the one hand, drinks are our lifeline:

they quench our thirst and keep us hydrated. On the other hand, they're basically liquid sugar bombs wrapped in artificial nonsense, contributing to the global obesity epidemic and environmental apocalypse. It's like they're saying, "Here, enjoy this deliciously toxic elixir that'll help you sink faster into your couch!"

As a self-proclaimed health nut, I find myself in a constant battle with my drink choices. But believe me, it's not just about the personal guilt of indulging in a sugary mess. No, no. It's about the full-blown chaos of being a delivery driver and trying to manage a delivery of four-plus fountain drinks. Imagine juggling those bad boys—it's like walking a tightrope with a tray of wobbly chemistry experiments. One wrong move and you've got a sticky soda disaster on your hands. But hey, I get it, the customer is just trying to hydrate. So, I grit my teeth and don't complain, all while mentally screaming, "Why do you need so many drinks?!"

And then we have the two-liter bottles. Oh, the two-liter bottles. They're the gift that keeps on giving—if that gift were a ticking time bomb. To a delivery driver, they're like carrying a grenade with a slow fuse. The chance of them leaking or exploding in the car is enough to make me want to shout, "Leave me alone!" Yet, they're the epitome of bulk-buying convenience. Seriously, who decided that having a half-gallon of soda for your Friday night movie was a good idea?

Now let's get to the ice-to-drink ratio. This is where I feel like a contestant on a game show: "Guess the Ice Level!" Too much ice and you've got a cup of slush; too little, and it's just a warm disappointment. It's a delicate balance that could either make someone's day or have them plotting your downfall. And mixing flavors? Oh, don't even get me started. It's like playing Russian roulette with a soda fountain. One minute you've got a delightful concoction, and the next you've brewed a disaster that tastes like regret.

And then there was the day a woman ordered a drink and asked me which cup size was "medium." My first thought was, "Are you serious?" It's like asking me to define what "average" means. I mean, how am I supposed to know her personal definition of medium? But, because the customer is always right—even when they're hopelessly vague—I took a deep breath and said, "Uh, the one that looks like it's in the middle." I felt a tiny pang of guilt for not being more precise, but hey, I was doing my best with the cosmic joke that is customer service.

Speaking of size, let's chat about straws. If you're in New Jersey, you now have to explicitly ask for a straw. Seriously? It's as if the law is saying, "Plastic bottles are fine, but plastic straws? Oh no, that's the real villain!" As a delivery driver, I'm caught between following the absurdity of the law and keeping my customers happy. The irony is not lost on me. It feels like the government is playing a twisted game, seeing how many pointless regulations they can throw at us before we break. I wouldn't be surprised if the person behind this straw madness is sitting somewhere, laughing their socks off at how ridiculously frustrating it all is.

In the end, drinks are a minefield of confusion and contradiction. From health dilemmas to customer satisfaction, from bizarre regulations to my own personal struggle, it's a tangled mess. But I trudge through, making the best of this liquid quagmire, even if that means rolling my eyes while I do it. Cheers to navigating this absurd world of drinks, one questionable sip at a time!

Chapter Four:
The Order And Delivery Situations: Where We Dive Deep Into Frustration, Your Etiquette Takes A Vacation, And The Cheese Invades Our Patience

Ah, the etiquette of ordering food. It's a marvel of modern civilization, yet somehow, it's become an enigma wrapped in a riddle for many. Let's break it down, shall we? You've ordered your food, and now you're in for the real treat: waiting. The cashier gives you a time frame, not as a whimsical guess but as a reality check. When they say 30 minutes on a Friday or Saturday, it's not because they're indulging in a secret hobby of making people wait. No, it's because the kitchen is drowning in a tidal wave of orders. Your staring contest with the counter won't speed things up. In fact, it'll only make the kitchen crew resent you more. Nothing screams, "I'm impatient," like your face pressed against the glass.

And let's talk about those magical moments when you arrive early, believing your premature presence will somehow warp time and space. Spoiler alert: It won't. The food isn't even in the oven yet, and if you glare hard enough, you might just get an extra helping of frustration from the staff. Your order is not sitting there, twiddling its thumbs, waiting for your grand entrance. It's probably still a mere thought in the chef's mind.

Now, if you're one of those who fancy adding a little something to your order at pick-up, don't expect the cashier to be your personal order tracker. If you think yelling out your request will magically pinpoint your order from the abyss of other orders, think again. The staff are juggling a million tasks and probably have no clue which one is yours. Just wait your turn, tell the cashier calmly, and they'll ring it up for you. Yes, that does mean you'll have to pay extra, but that's a whole different story.

And speaking of forgetfulness, let's discuss the joy of customers who forget their order numbers. It's as if they believe the world revolves around their inability to remember three simple digits. When they blame us for their slip-ups, it's a special kind of frustrating. We're here trying to keep the line moving, but your memory lapses are throwing us off course. On busy nights, we hand out order numbers to keep things organized. It's not a secret code or a test of your memory. Remember your number and your food will come to you faster. It's not rocket science.

For those who believe they're too important for order numbers and prefer to just blurt out their name, here's a newsflash: there are more than a few Johns and Marys in our system. We can't magically divine your order from thin air. And yes, it's a tad inconvenient when we have to search through the chaos to find yours. It's like playing a game of "Find the

Needle in the Haystack," except the haystack is made up of a hundred orders and your name is just one needle.

But don't worry, the fun doesn't end with your forgetfulness. We also have those stellar individuals who call back, claiming their food is late when it's not. First off, there's the classic "I've been waiting forever" complaint. Look, we have fancy computers that track every blink of your order's eye. So, when you call us and claim your food has been circling the earth for an hour, we know you're not exactly telling the truth. It's like watching a rerun of the same tired soap opera: we know exactly how long you've been waiting because we're the ones juggling your order. But oh no, we can't call you out on your little fib. Instead, we plaster on our best fake sympathy and apologize for the "inconvenience."

And then there's the next level of entitlement. Let me tell you about the woman who took "demanding" to new heights. Our phones went down for a few minutes—something entirely out of our control. But instead of waiting it out like a reasonable person, she somehow tracked down my boss's cell phone number and placed the order with him. And mind you, it was his day off. So, when I dropped off her delivery, I did what anyone would do: I apologized for the delay and casually mentioned how someone bothered my boss on his day off, nearly got the poor manager fired (complete lie, by the way, the other owner was working). But hey, a little guilt trip never hurt anyone, right? Maybe next time, she'll think twice before being such a snobby pain in the ass.

Then we have the real treat: customers who refuse to listen. They spout off their orders like they're reciting Shakespeare and expect us to catch every word. "Did you want fries with that?" "Oh, I don't know. I just thought you'd know." Really? How is it our fault when your order morphs into a half-eaten mess of regret? If only we had a magic crystal ball to see into your culinary dreams.

And oh, the weather! Those days when we're battling snow to falling rain or hailing frogs to the blazing sun just to get your food to you. It's almost poetic, really. We're out there risking life and limb to deliver your meal, and yet, you're complaining because it's a few minutes late. Do you not realize we're out there, braving the elements so you can enjoy your pizza in the comfort of your warm, dry home? But do you appreciate it? Of course not. Instead, you're on the phone moaning about how your pizza is "taking forever." Sure, we could have stayed cozy by the fire, but no, we're out here dodging icicles for your extra cheese.

And then, there is the joy of navigating your treacherous driveways, sidewalks, and porches. Ever tried delivering food through a snowbank or over an ice rink? It's like being part of a poorly planned obstacle course. But hey, don't worry about shoveling, it's no biggie, don't even bother to clear your driveways. Just sit back, relax, and make sure to call us later to complain that your food is "late." Because clearly, we're equipped to handle the Arctic tundra and your messy front yard with nothing but a thin layer of plastic wrap. Honestly, guys, what do you expect us to do? Skateboard your pizza to your door?

Now, let's discuss timing. If you're not ready when we arrive, do you really want to be caught in your pajamas with bedhead? Is that the impression you want to make? But hey, if you're not prepared, it's our fault. We'll just wait forever because, apparently, we have all the time in the world to stand around while you finish your beauty sleep.

Ever had a driver call you and get no response? It's like a silent film—no dialogue, just a lot of frantic knocking and phone calls. And when you don't answer, don't expect us to stick around. We'll leave with your food faster than you can say, "forgot to set the alarm."

And then there's the "I fell asleep" excuse. Really? Did you think your food would magically stay hot while you snooze? Well, guess what? Your nap isn't going to magically make us reheat your food for free. Next time, try to stay awake—your hunger will thank you.

Now, let's talk about pets. Yes, the loveable canines and furry creatures who have no concept of boundaries and are the cause of more chaos. Please, for the sake of everyone's sanity, keep your dogs inside when we arrive. Some people might be terrified of dogs, or worse, your furry friend might decide that the delivery driver's car is their new playground. We're not interested in playing fetch or dealing with a four-legged barricade. And if you've got one of those "friendly" but overly enthusiastic dogs? Brace yourself. We're not here for the puppy show. Imagine our surprise when we open the door to find a dog lounging in the front seat. It's cute but also mildly terrifying when you're on a schedule.

Speaking of things that throw a wrench in our gears, let's address the elephant in the room: GrubHub and DoorDash. These guys are like the annoying cousins who show up at every family gathering and somehow manage to eat all the food without bringing anything to the table. They want us to sign up, take 30% of our profit, and still expect us to smile about it. Um, no thanks. We're not even making a 30% profit on most orders, so it's more like paying them to take our money. And let's not forget their 'generous' markups—they give you a stripped-down version of our menu, jack up the prices, and we all end up getting ripped off. So, please, for the love of all that's holy (and tasty), steer clear of them. Do it for the restaurants across the nation that are trying to survive without being bled dry by these middlemen.

On another note, why are ketchup and other condiments such a big deal for deliveries? We get it, and you might need some extra ketchup. But is it really too much to ask to have a little stash at home? It's not that we don't want to give you extra condiments; it's just that we've got a limited supply and an even more limited budget. If you're too lazy to get ketchup from your fridge, maybe consider this: we're not your personal condiment fairy. Especially when you can't even tip us enough for what we already provide!

Now, on to the delicate matter of tipping. We operate within a five-mile radius for deliveries. Sometimes, we have two or three deliveries heading in the same direction, and usually, we drop them off in the order they come in. But here's the thing: if you're one of those folks who either doesn't tip or thinks a handful of pennies counts as "enough," you might find yourself waiting a little longer. We're not saying your food will be cold, just that the driver might prioritize the customer who understands the value of a good tip. It's a simple equation, really: decent tip equals quicker service. It's beyond frustrating to drive five miles to the edge of our delivery area, burn through gas, and then be greeted with a dollar or, worse, a pile of loose change. If you can't afford to tip at least $3.00, maybe consider picking up your order yourself. Honestly, $5.00 is the sweet spot, but if you're just around the corner, we'll graciously accept $3.00.

In conclusion, the delivery world is a circus of mixed signals, unreasonable demands, and endless patience. We trudge through it all, hoping for a little understanding and maybe a smile along the way. So next time you're on the other side of the door, remember: We're juggling a lot more than just your food.

And here's the takeaway: be considerate. Remember your order number, clear your walkways, keep your pets inside, and maybe think twice before blaming us for things beyond our control. We're doing our best, juggling a million things and trying to make sure your food gets to you as quickly as possible. It's not a perfect system, but with a little bit of patience and understanding, we might just make this whole food delivery experience a bit more pleasant for everyone involved.

Chapter Five:
The Great Customer Showdown: Complaining Your Way Out Of A Good Meal

There's a pervasive myth in the world of retail and service industries: "The customer is always right." It's an adage that's been pounded into the heads of countless employees, used as a cudgel to justify every unreasonable demand, every outrageous complaint, every unwarranted temper tantrum thrown over something as trivial as an extra packet of sauce. But let me tell you something – and I'll be blunt here – that is complete bullshit.

Yes, I said it. And if you've ever worked a single day in customer service, deep down, you know it too. The customer isn't always right. In fact, some of them are insufferably wrong, and it's about time we start calling it like it is.

Let's start with those customers who seem to derive pleasure from making everyone else miserable. They walk in with a chip on their shoulder, looking for the slightest reason to unleash their pent-up frustrations on some poor, unsuspecting worker. They're the ones who complain before they've even given the food a chance, who nitpick every detail of the service, who seem to believe that the world owes them something just because they showed up.

Take, for instance, the customer who gave our cashier a hard time about her tie-dye shirt. He waltzed in, took one look at her, and decided that her choice of clothing meant she must be some kind of unpatriotic drug user. The ignorance and prejudice rolled off him in waves as he ranted and raved, and it was clear he was itching for a fight. Our cashier, bless her heart, stood her ground and called him out on his rudeness. Of course, the man didn't have the emotional maturity to accept that. He turned to my boss, expecting backup for his absurd worldview, only to be met with a firm, "You started it. She has a right to respond."

And you know what? That's exactly how it should be. No one has the right to talk down to others, no matter who they are. My boss, in a show of solidarity, ordered tie-dye uniform shirts for the whole crew. We wore them proudly, a silent middle finger to the bigots of the world. Unsurprisingly, that customer never showed his face again. And honestly, good riddance.

In the cutthroat world of corporate retail, firing a customer is almost unheard of. I mean, workers are meant to be fired, not customers, right? The prevailing wisdom is that every customer is valuable and that every dollar is worth the price of enduring whatever abuse is thrown our way.

But here's the thing: some customers have truly made it their life's sole purpose to challenge that idea.

My bosses – bless them for their wisdom – have fired more than one customer in their time. It's not something they do lightly, but when someone consistently causes trouble, makes unreasonable demands, or treats the staff like garbage, it's time to show them the door.

One repeat offender in particular comes to mind – a man who always asked for extra sauce on his wings but never wanted to pay for it. He'd call back after every order, claiming there wasn't enough sauce, even though we made sure to practically drown his wings in it. It became a running joke among the staff, with everyone watching to make sure his order was perfect just so we could call him out on his lies.

Eventually, my boss had enough. He told the man straight up, "If we can never get your order right, maybe you should take your order elsewhere." For a month, we didn't hear from him. But as they say, absence makes the heart grow fonder – or in his case, the stomach hungrier. He came crawling back, unable to resist the lure of our delicious food. We let him order again, but the message was clear: we're not here to be taken advantage of.

Now, let me get something straight: we in the service industry aren't perfect. We make mistakes. We have off days. But for the most part, we bust our asses to make sure the food is good, the service is prompt, and the customers leave happy. And yet, there's this odd phenomenon where people think it's okay to mess with the very folks who are preparing their meals. Have they not heard, "Do not bite the hand that feeds you"?

Let me put this in perspective: we're the ones handling your food. We can make it the best damn meal you've ever had, or we can make it the stuff of nightmares. We can follow the order of tickets, or we can "accidentally" misplace yours. So why on earth would anyone think it's a good idea to treat us poorly?

For those of you who think you're better than us, let me tell you something – 90% of you wouldn't last a day in our shoes. You wouldn't be able to handle the fast pace, the constant pressure, and the chaos that comes with trying to please a dozen people at once. And yet, you waltz in, thinking you can do our job better, thinking you're entitled to special treatment. Here's a suggestion: spend a week working in a restaurant. I guarantee your attitude will change.

There's another breed of customer that's almost worse than the chronic complainers – the entitled ones. These are the folks who think the rules don't apply to them, who believe they can bend reality to suit their whims. They genuinely thing the world revolves around them and their oversized egos.

I'll give you a prime example: the woman who loves to order two minutes before we close. Not only does she place her order at the last possible second, but she also has the audacity to order something ridiculously specific and annoying – a buffalo stromboli with no cheese. For those who aren't familiar, that's basically just chicken, sauce, and dough. It's tiny, it's a pain to make, and she doesn't even have the decency to pick it up on time. She'd show up half an hour late, leaving us stuck at the shop long after we should've been home.

After the third time, we had enough. We stopped answering the phone at 9:50 p.m. sharp. Call it rude if you want, but we're human beings too, and we deserve to go home on time just like everyone else.

And then there are the afterthought requests – those infuriating moments when a customer suddenly remembers they want something on the side after they've already paid. Now, I'm not talking about the honest ones, the folks who genuinely forgot and are willing to pay for the extra item. No, I'm talking about the ones who do it on purpose, who think they can get one over on us, who seem to believe that they're entitled to freebies just because they're customers.

To those people, let me be clear: we see you. We know exactly who you are, and we're tired of your games. We're not here to be taken advantage of. We're not here to give away freebies. We're here to make a living, just like you. And when we charge you for that extra side of honey mustard, don't act surprised. Don't try to haggle or negotiate. It's not going to work. No refunds in this spot!

You see, we don't get anything for free. Our suppliers charge us for everything, and if we started giving things away, we'd be out of business in no time. And then where would you be? So take your entitled attitude and your penny-pinching ways somewhere else. We don't have time for it.

Working in the service industry isn't for the faint of heart. It's a grind, day in and day out, dealing with all sorts of personalities, from the kind and considerate to the downright despicable. But there's a camaraderie that forms among the staff, a shared understanding that we're all in this together. We have each other's backs because, quite frankly, if we didn't, we'd be overwhelmed by the sheer volume of nonsense we have to deal with.

And that's something the customers don't always see. They don't see the behind-the-scenes chaos, the juggling act we perform to keep everything running smoothly. They don't see the frustration when someone's order gets messed up, the scramble to fix it, the relief when it's finally sorted. All they see is the end result – the food on their plate, the drink in their hand, the smile on their faces.

But just because they don't see it doesn't mean it's not there. And just because we're smiling doesn't mean we're not fed up with your crap. So the next time you think about giving your server a hard time, remember this: we're doing our best. And if you push us too far, don't be surprised if you find yourself looking for a new place to eat.

Now, I don't want you to think that all customers are terrible. Far from it. In fact, most of them are downright lovely. They're the ones who make this job worthwhile, who remind us why we show up every day, and who treat us with the respect and kindness we deserve.

There's the regular who orders the same thing every time – predictable, sure, but always polite, always grateful. There's the family who comes in every Friday night, the kids excited to see us, the parents happy to chat for a few minutes. There's the elderly couple who split a meal, who always leave a generous tip and thank us for our service.

These are the customers we live for, the ones who make all the nonsense worthwhile. They're the reason we put up with the complainers, the entitled, and the afterthought-requesters. Because for every one of them, there's someone who makes our day a little brighter, who reminds us that not everyone is out to make our lives difficult.

So to those customers – you know who you are – thank you. Thank you for being decent human beings. Thank you for treating us with respect. Thank you for understanding that we're people too, just trying to do our jobs the best we can.

The reality of customer service is this: it's not glamorous, it's not easy, and it's not always fair. But it's a job that teaches you a lot about people – the good, the bad, and the downright ugly. It teaches you patience, resilience, and, most importantly, the ability to stand up for yourself and your coworkers.

So the next time you walk into a restaurant, a store, or any place where someone is there to serve you, remember this: they're not your punching bag. They're not there to take your abuse. They're there to do a job, and they deserve your respect.

Because at the end of the day, the customer isn't always right. And sometimes, they need to be reminded of that.

Chapter Six:
The Art Of Free Food Schemes, Timed Orders, And The Sauce Saga

Running a restaurant is like trying to herd cats while juggling flaming swords—only with more grease and the constant risk of third-degree burns. And believe me, it's not as glamorous as it sounds. Behind the scenes, it's a warzone where the enemy is time, the battlefield is the kitchen, and the casualties are your sanity.

Imagine this: the sizzle of the grill, the smell of freshly baked bread wafting through the air, and the frantic dance of cooks trying not to trip over each other as they hustle to get everything perfect. It's a symphony of chaos, and if we can make it through a single day without setting off the fire alarms, we're practically miracle workers. But just when we think we've mastered the art of orchestrating this culinary circus, along comes a customer who's determined to act like the circus clown and throw a wrench—or maybe a ladle—into our well-oiled machine.

Now, we're not saying that we're perfect. Mistakes happen—like when a cheese steak hoagie magically morphs into a steak hoagie. It's a simple error, and we're more than happy to fix it. All we ask is that you send it back to us so we can see the crime scene with our own eyes. You'd think that would be common sense, right? But no, some people seem to believe we have psychic powers and can fix their order with just a bit of telepathic mumbo jumbo. Spoiler alert: we can't.

Yet, despite our willingness to make things right, there are those who think they can outsmart us. They'll call up, sometimes the next day, and sometimes even weeks later, complaining about their order and demanding a free meal. And when we ask them to return the wrong food, they suddenly have a change of heart. "Oh, I already ate it," they say as if they expect us to pat them on the back and send them a new meal on the house. Nice try, Sherlock, but that's not how it works. We're not running a charity here; we're running a business, and contrary to popular belief, we actually keep track of who's trying to pull a fast one on us.

Just the other day, we had a guy who ordered a $60 meal and then had the audacity to claim there should have been two pizzas when our records clearly showed only one. We were more than willing to whip up another pizza for him, but he would have to pay for it. Well, that didn't sit well with him. He threw a tantrum that would give a spoiled toddler an inferiority complex, screaming and cursing at our cashier, before ultimately deciding to send all the food back because he didn't get his way. Bravo, sir. Truly a masterclass in maturity.

I often wonder how people like this treat their own families and friends. I can only imagine the chaos that must ensue during Thanksgiving dinner. "What do you mean there's only one turkey? I distinctly remember ordering two!" And then the poor host is left with a half-eaten bird and a lot of questions. At least they get to have a funny story to tell their friends in the eventual future.

But it's not just the freeloaders that make this job a test of patience. Let's talk about timed orders. The mere mention of them sends a shiver down my spine. The idea is simple enough: you need your food at a specific time because lunch breaks are short and precious. Fair enough. But here's where it gets tricky: Some folks seem to think that ordering two slices of pizza or a hoagie two hours in advance is a good idea. I mean, really? You do realize these things take minutes to prepare, not hours, right? But no, they insist on ordering ahead and then show up early, staring at us like we're going to make their food cook faster through sheer fear or willpower. Sorry to disappoint, but your intense gaze isn't going to speed up the process. Your order will be ready when you asked for it, not a minute before, not a minute after. It's called a timed order for a reason, folks.

And then there's the art of pre-ordering. In theory, it's a fantastic idea. You call ahead, we get a heads up, and everyone's happy. But in practice? It's a double-edged sword that's been giving us a collective migraine since COVID-19 hit. Before the pandemic, a big pre-order was maybe 10 or 15 pizzas and a hundred wings. Annoying, sure, but manageable. But now? Now we're dealing with individual sandwich orders for every single employee because apparently, no one is allowed to touch each other's food anymore. Each sandwich has to be packed separately, with its own napkin, ketchup, and whatever else. It's like packing a hundred individual lunch boxes for a field trip to stress-land that you never even signed up for.

Take, for example, the car dealership that pre-ordered 75 sandwiches. They gave us the order the day before, which was a godsend, but then they asked for it at 12 noon on a Friday. Talk about perfect timing to drive us to the brink of madness. And don't even get me started on the skydiving place down the street. The old owners used to pre-order 60 to 80 pizzas once a month. Now that is an order that needs to be pre-ordered. But then there are people who will pre-order just two pizzas. Really? We appreciate the gesture, but it's not necessary to order that far in advance. Just call us when you're on your way, and we'll have it ready for you in a jiffy.

So here's the deal: if your order is over $150 or has more than fifteen different items, please, for the love of all things sane, give us some advance notice. Call us the day before or at least a couple of hours ahead. We'll make sure your food is ready on time, and you won't have to deal with a bunch of grumpy kitchen staff who were forced to pull off the culinary equivalent of a miracle. Your stomachs and our sanity will thank you.

Now, let's talk about sauce. Yes, sauce. The lifeblood of any good wing order. But seriously, why do you need four cups of mild sauce, four cups of blue cheese, and four cups of ranch for a measly six wings? That's more liquid than chicken at that point. And at 75 cents a pop, it's not exactly cheap either. How about we all just agree to be a little more reasonable with our sauce requests? Buy a bottle of each, and we'll all be a lot happier.

While we're on the subject of specials, let me drop some knowledge on you. Lunch specials are only valid from 11 a.m. to 3 p.m. That's four hours out of the entire day. They're called "specials" for a reason, people. They're not meant to be available all day, every day. And let's not forget about our daily specials, like the buy-one-hoagie-get-the-second-half-price deal on Wednesdays. Now, that's a deal worth waiting for. But if we were to offer that or any other special every single day, it would no longer be special. It would just be our everyday price, which, by the way, is already too low for us to stay afloat. We've got employees to pay, suppliers to keep happy, and overhead costs that could sink a small ship. So, please, stop asking for specials every time you order. They're called "specials" for a reason—let's keep it that way.

And while I have your attention, let's talk about ordering from or for a business. If you're ordering for a large facility, like a car dealership with multiple departments, please do us all a favor and give your name and the section you're in. It saves so much time and energy when our delivery drivers don't have to play a game of hide-and-seek to find you. And for the love of all things efficient, stop splitting the bill. When a small glasses store makes us create three separate orders for the same place, it's annoying beyond belief. Not only does it create unnecessary complications, but it also means you're all paying extra delivery charges. Why not just figure out who owes what and combine it into one order? It's simple, it saves money, and it keeps our precious drivers from losing their minds.

And while we're at it, let's address the Wal-Marts of the world. People will order food and then promptly vanish, leaving our drivers wandering around like lost puppies for 15 minutes trying to find them. Here's a pro tip: leave the money with the customer service department. It's a small action that saves everyone time and frustration. It's gotten so bad that our drivers will sometimes have to leave with the food, make other deliveries, and come back later. Of course, this upsets the Wal-Mart employees, but we're not about to let one person's delay affect all our other deliveries. So please, be considerate and make sure someone is available to accept the order when our drivers arrive.

I get it, most people prefer to use credit cards these days. But there are other ways to pay without causing delays. How about taking turns paying, or using Venmo to transfer money between colleagues? It's just a small adjustment that can greatly improve the efficiency of our deliveries.

Let's all work together to make ordering from or for a business a smoother, more enjoyable experience. Remember to state your location, combine orders to save money, and be considerate of our delivery drivers. With these simple changes, we can all save time, energy, and a few strands of our already thinning hair. Thank you for your cooperation.

And now, let's get back to the real reason we're all here: Enjoying some mouth-watering food, preferably without a side of stress and a dipping of annoyance.

Chapter Seven:
Eggplants, Egos, And Eccentricities

Running a restaurant is like stepping into a never-ending carnival of the bizarre and unpredictable. Every day brings a fresh wave of chaos, and you never quite know what flavor of madness you'll be dealing with. It's a whirlwind of personalities, cravings, and collective behaviors that defy all logic and reason. Take, for instance, the phenomenon we've come to dub "the collective consciousness of cravings." It's one of the most perplexing, yet strangely fascinating, aspects of our daily operations.

Picture this: we can go an entire week without selling a single eggplant parm sandwich. The eggplants sit there, unassuming, waiting for their moment in the sun. Then, out of the blue, a switch is flipped, and suddenly, in the span of one day, we'll sell eight of them. It's as if the universe sent out a memo, and our customers all decided, independently, that today is the day for eggplant parm. And it's not just the sandwiches—

oh no, this phenomenon extends to everything on our menu. It's like our customers are all connected on some deeper level, influencing each other's choices without even realizing it. How else can you explain the inexplicable surge in demand for a particular dish on a random Tuesday?

And it doesn't stop there. The timing of these orders is just as mysterious. Typically, our lunch rush falls between 11:30 a.m. and 1:30 p.m., with the peak around noon. But every so often, a new trend emerges out of nowhere. Suddenly, it's like our customers have collectively decided that 2 p.m. is the new lunchtime. The kitchen is caught off guard, the servers are scrambling, and we're all left wondering what cosmic force is at play. Is there some hidden network of communication among our patrons? Are there whispers and murmurs spreading through the grapevine, nudging them to order at the same time? Or is it just a strange quirk of fate, one we'll never fully understand?

Whatever the cause, this collective consciousness of cravings adds an extra layer of unpredictability to an already chaotic environment. Our customers, bless their hearts, are an enigmatic bunch. Some are creatures of habit, sticking to the same order every time like it's a sacred ritual. Others are spontaneous and adventurous, eager to try something new with every visit. And then there are those who seem to have an unspoken connection with our restaurant, always knowing the perfect time to drop in for a quick bite or a leisurely meal. It's almost as if our customers have their own unique personalities, each with their own quirks and preferences. We can't help but feel a sense of kinship with them as we navigate this mysterious world together.

But let's not romanticize it too much—working in the restaurant industry also means dealing with a fair share of sheer absurdity. And let me tell you, I've encountered some real gems in my time as a server. These stories will make you question the sanity of some individuals, and they're too good not to share.

First, let's talk about the woman who would order a salad, but not just any salad. She was "highly allergic" to tomatoes and made sure we knew it. Fair enough—food allergies are no joke. But here's the kicker: as she waited for her order, she'd sit there, happily munching on a slice of pizza. Tomato sauce, anyone? The audacity! It boggled my mind every time. How do you square that circle?

Then there was the lady who called in a fit of rage, claiming there was mold in her blue cheese. Let that sink in for a moment—mold in blue cheese. Yes, ma'am, that's kind of the point. But this woman was so incensed, she couldn't see the absurdity of her complaint. She was ready to start a war over it. And let's not forget the customer who called back, fuming because there were preservatives on their roast beef. Preservatives. On roast beef. As if that's some kind of shocking revelation. I had to bite my tongue not to laugh. "Sorry, sir, but I'm pretty sure it's called 'preserved' beef for a reason."

Oh, and here's a real gem. A man called in, seething with anger because we forgot to include a cup of cheese with his order. He was so livid that he actually made our poor cashier cry. That's when I stepped in and took the phone from her. I calmly explained to the man that he was threatening a minor and that the police were on their way to his house. Needless to say, he didn't have much to say after that.

But the most mind-boggling customer of all? This guy who claimed to be "terrified" of COVID. And yet, when he came into the restaurant, he chose to sit at the only table that had other customers. I mean, seriously? There were five other tables available, and he chose the one next to other people? It's like these customers are playing a game of "who can be the most illogical and irrational." Honestly, sometimes I question my own sanity working in this industry. The things people do just defy all common sense. But I know one thing for sure—I will always stand up for myself and my coworkers. We are human beings, and we will not tolerate being treated with disrespect. So to all the crazy customers out there, I have one message for you—don't mess with us.

And let's not forget the coupon saga. Ah, the elusive coupon. There was this one woman, desperate for a deal, who constantly ordered delivery and insisted she had a coupon. Her voice, shrill and persistent, echoed through the phone as she demanded contactless delivery. We obliged, instructing her to leave the coupon in the mailbox or on the porch. But then, she confessed her sister actually possessed the coupon and she was in Michigan! And would you believe it, another time it was all the way in Delaware. That coupon has traveled to more places than I have! We diligently collect these elusive coupons because they are for one use only. It's just like our specials, only available on certain days or times. If we didn't collect them, you'd be getting discounted food all the time. It would no longer be a special treat, but a cheap, everyday occurrence. And don't even think about trying to cheat the system by making copies. We're not that naive.

And then there's another special kind of customer, one that every restaurant dreads. And no, I'm not just talking about the ones who insist on ordering their pizza with twelve different toppings, half of which we probably don't even have in stock. I'm talking about the sneaky ones—the thieves. Now, I know you're thinking, "Stealing? In a restaurant? Who does that?" But you'd be surprised. Some people will pocket anything that isn't nailed down, and I'm not just talking about the leftover breadsticks.

You see, we've had our fair share of mysterious disappearances around here. Silverware? Gone without a trace. Toilet paper? Vanished into thin air. I kid you not, we've had customers make off with more than just their to-go boxes. One time, an entire roll of toilet paper just disappeared from the bathroom, and we were left scratching our heads, wondering if someone had really stuffed it into their bag. And the silverware? Forget about it. We've lost more forks and knives than I can count. It's like people think it's complimentary, like the bread or the extra napkins.

Now, I know these items might seem insignificant, but when you run a restaurant, these little losses add up. And while it might seem harmless to slip an extra fork into your purse, it's just another headache for the staff who already have their hands full trying to keep things running smoothly. So, if you ever catch yourself thinking that a fork or roll of toilet paper would make a nice souvenir, do us all a favor—leave it where it belongs. Trust me, it'll make your pizza experience a whole lot smoother, and the staff will be grateful you didn't add to their list of daily mysteries.

But let's not forget the real characters in this story—the hardworking employees who tirelessly take your orders and deliver your food. They, like the rest of us, are not immune to the allure of a good deal. But they also understand the value of hard work and the importance of following the rules. They are the unsung heroes in this chaotic world of coupons and discounts. So next time you order delivery, remember the journey that coupon has taken and the people who make it all possible. And maybe, just maybe, tip a little extra to show your appreciation for their dedication and integrity. Because in a world filled with cheats and scammers, it's refreshing to know there are still honest, hardworking individuals out there.

Now, let me tell you about a tip-related incident that still gets under my skin. It was a delivery to a school, a familiar stop on our route. But this time, a new face greeted me with the money. It was a teacher, and she meticulously counted out the payment before keeping $8 as a tip. Eight measly dollars. That's our usual tip, but she actually kept it for herself! I was dumbfounded. What a heartless, selfish bitch. I needed to spread the word to the other teachers and let them know what kind of person this woman truly was. My boss assured me he would handle it, but it still left a bitter taste in my mouth. How could someone be so callous and deceitful?

As if that wasn't enough, a woman called back in a fit of rage. She was irate that there was blood on her receipt. Can you believe it? She actually had the audacity to yell at us for having an employee bleed on her food. But here's the kicker—there was no blood. Our printer tape just happened to have a red streak on it, signaling that it was running low. But this woman, she was a nut case. Jumping to conclusions and causing a scene over nothing. It's moments like these that make me question humanity. How can people be so cruel and irrational? It's beyond me. But I'll keep delivering, keep encountering these characters, and keep using my rich, colorful voice to tell their stories. Because let's face it, the world is full of interesting and complex characters, and I wouldn't have it any other way.

After a particularly rough day, I decided to discuss these bizarre experiences with people who worked in different types of restaurants. If you think my tales are wild, you should hear what goes on in sit-down restaurants. The stories they told me were enough to make anyone's head spin.

Let's start with reservations. Some places accept them, and some don't. Some places do call-ahead seating, where you can join the current waitlist but can't choose a specific time to come in and eat. And you wouldn't believe the audacity of some customers. They'll complain about long wait times, all the while being the same people who will sit at a table for three hours, creating those long wait times in the first place! And here's a public service announcement: if you're waiting to be seated, please, for the love of all that is holy, don't let your children run around and scream. Take them outside and let them burn off that energy. And if you see an older customer or someone who looks like they need it, let them sit while you stand. It's just common decency.

And if you're one of those people who think a 10-minute wait is too long, consider this: it's the same time it takes you to wait for your food at a fast food joint, which you have no problem with. And let me tell you, we can't guarantee that a certain table will be available when you arrive. We can't force people to leave, and we can't make them eat faster. We're not wizards! So if you want to be seated right away, come early. Otherwise, suck it up and wait like everyone else.

Speaking of fast food, let me clarify something. A sit-down restaurant is not fast food. The wait times are longer because we're making your food to order. That takes time. So don't come in with the expectation that you'll be in and out in 15 minutes. And for the love of God, don't treat us like we're androids without lives of our own. We're not here to serve you as quickly as possible so you can go about your day. We're here to provide a dining experience, and that takes time. So sit back, relax, and enjoy the atmosphere.

And here's another thing: don't come in with a party of 20 and expect to be seated right away. We need time to prepare a table for that many people, and we can't just kick other customers out to make room for you. It's common sense! If you know you're coming with a large group, call ahead and let us know. We'll do our best to accommodate you but don't expect miracles. And if we can't seat you right away, don't take it out on the host or hostess. They're just doing their job.

And here's a tip for everyone: be polite. If you come in with a smile and a friendly attitude, you're more likely to get better service. We're human beings, and we respond to kindness. If you're rude and demanding, don't be surprised if your service is less than stellar. We're not robots; we have feelings, and we're more inclined to go the extra mile for someone who treats us with respect.

So the next time you're in a restaurant, whether it's a fast food or a sit-down establishment, remember that we're all just trying to do our jobs. We're here to provide you with a meal and a dining experience, but we're not miracle workers. We can't control everything, and we're not perfect. So be patient, be kind, and tip generously. And if you do, you might just have a dining experience that's as enjoyable for us as it is for you.

Chapter Eight:
The Last Slice: How To Order Like A Pro And Keep Everyone Happy

Now that we have spent the whole book lamenting about our wacky experiences and bizarre encounters, let's talk about something near and dear to every server's heart: the proper way to order food. If you've made it this far in the book, you've probably picked up on the fact that there's a right way and a wrong way to do just about everything in the restaurant world. Ordering is no different. The way you approach that simple task can either make our lives a little easier—or drive us absolutely up the wall. And believe me, we've seen it all.

Let's start with the right way. It's the stuff of dreams for anyone who has ever worked in food service. The customer who calls in knows exactly what they want, orders it in one go, confirms the details when we read it back, and then simply waits for their food to arrive. Beautiful. It's the kind of interaction that restores our faith in humanity, even if just for a moment.

Right Way:

- Us: "Hi, is this for pick-up or delivery?"

- Customer: "Delivery."

- Us: "Is your address still 123 Main Street?"

- Customer: "Yes, it is."

- Us: "Great! What can I get for you today?"

- Customer: "I'd like a large pizza, half plain, half pepperoni, and a BBQ chicken pizza."

- Us: "Anything else?"

- Customer: "Nope, that's all."

- Us: "Perfect. Your total is such-and-such, and we'll be there in about 30 to 40 minutes."

- Customer: "Thanks!"

- Us: "You're welcome. Have a good day!"

Now that, my friends, is how it's done. No fuss, no complications—just a straightforward order that gets processed quickly and delivered without a hitch. But, oh, how rare these moments are. For every smooth, easy order, there are a dozen others that are anything but. Enter the wrong way.

Wrong Way:

- Us: "Hi, is this for pick-up or delivery?"

- Customer: "Delivery."

- Us: "Is your address still 123 Main Street?"

- Customer: "Yes, it is."

- Us: "Great! What can I get for you today?"

- Customer: "I'd like a large pizza, half plain, half pepperoni, and a BBQ chicken pizza."

- Us: "Anything else?"

- Customer: "No, that's all."

- Us: "Perfect. Your total is such-and-such, and we'll be there in about 30 to 40 minutes."

- Customer: "Oh, by the way, can I add onions to the BBQ pizza?"

- Us: "Just a minute, I have to re-enter that."

- Customer: (20 minutes later) "Hey, can I add chicken fingers and fries to that? Oh, and a cheesesteak, too."

- Us: "Sure, just a minute to enter that. Anything on the cheesesteak?"

- Customer: "Yes, some onions."

- Us: "Fried or raw?"

- Customer: "Fried."

- Us: "Any honey mustard or BBQ sauce for the chicken?"

- Customer: "No, but can I have buffalo sauce?"

- Us: "Which flavor—mild, medium, or hot?"

- Customer: "Mild."

- Us: "Anything else?"

- Customer: "No."

- Us: (Reads back the order again.)

- Customer: (No response.)

- Us: "Ok, see you soon."

In my head, I'm saying: "How do you forget you need this much stuff? You're driving me nuts!" But out loud, I just say, "Ok, we'll see you soon." Ah, the joys of customer service.

And it's not just phone orders. In-person orders can be just as maddening.

Right Way:

- Us: "Hi, is this for here or to go?"
- Customer: "For here."
- Customer: "I would like 2 slices of plain pizza and an order of cheese fries."
- Us: "Cheese on or on the side?"
- Customer: "On."
- Us: "Anything else?"
- Customer: "Yes, a medium fountain coke."
- Us: "Sure, let me get that for you, just a minute." (Comes back with the drink.) "Is that all?"
- Customer: "Yes."
- Us: (Reads back the order.)
- Customer: "Yup, that's it."
- Us: "Ok, your total is such-and-such. I will bring it out as soon as it is ready."
- Customer: "OK, thanks."

Wrong Way:

- Us: "Hi, is this for here or to go?"

- Customer: "For here."

- Customer: "I would like 2 slices of plain pizza and an order of cheese fries."

- Us: "Cheese on or on the side?"

- Customer: "On."

- Us: "Anything else?"

- Customer: "Yes, a medium fountain coke."

- Us: "Sure, let me get that for you, just a minute." (Comes back with the drink.)

- Customer: (After paying) "Oh, can I have a side of honey mustard and put the cheese on the side?"

- Us: "Sure, that will be 75 cents, and let me see if the fries are already done."

In my head, I'm thinking: "Because you're not getting anything free, and those fries are probably already drenched."

Then there are the wing orders. Oh, the wing orders.

Right Way:

- Us: "Hi, is this for pick-up or delivery?"
- Customer: "Pick-up."
- Us: "Ok, for [your name], what can I get for you?"
- Customer: "I would like 12 mild wings with blue cheese on the side."
- Us: "Ok, anything else?"
- Customer: "Yes, I would also like an order of curly fries."
- Us: "Ok, is that everything?"
- Customer: "Yes."
- Us: (Reads back the order.)
- Customer: "Yes, that's it."
- Us: "It is such-and-such price, and it will be ready in about 15 minutes."
- Customer: "Ok, thanks."

Wrong Way:

- Customer: "I would like 12 wings."
- Us: "Ok, what flavor?"
- Customer: "What are your flavors?"
- Us: (Reads them all.)
- Customer: "Give me medium and garlic parm mixed, make sure they're crispy."
- Us: "Sure, but they won't stay crispy once they're put in a container. Do you want the sauce on the side?"
- Customer: "No, put the sauce on them."
- Us: (In head: Don't call back complaining they weren't crispy.)
- Us: "Anything else?"
- Customer: "Yeah, curly fries."
- Us: "Ok, anything else?"
- Customer: "Put salt, pepper, and ketchup on those fries."
- Us: (In head: Really, you can't do that yourself?)
- Us: "Is that it?"
- Customer: "Yeah, I guess."

- Us: (In head: What do you mean you guess? Are you going to be calling back with more? Or are you just miserable? Ugh, you're driving me nuts!)

But you know what? For every difficult customer, there's a decent one that reminds me why I don't throw in the towel. The ones who get it—who understand that we're human beings trying to do our best. The ones who don't act like the world revolves around them, who are polite and grateful for the service we provide. And let me tell you, those customers make all the difference. They're the ones who make this chaotic job worth it.

I'd like to take a moment to thank them. They're my favorite regulars, the ones who make me smile every time they walk through the door. First, there's the older couple who always order a slice of sausage and a slice of white veggie, and they share a drink. They don't need much, just their simple order and each other's company, and that's what makes them so special. Then there are the three teachers who can't get enough of our buffalo chicken salad and wing zing pizza with blue cheese. They never get onions on their salad because they're heading back to teach, and the last thing they want is to knock out their students with onion breath. Thoughtful, right?

And let's not forget the couple who always got a cup of cheese with their chips while waiting for their Italian hoagie with extra onions. They knew what they wanted, and they enjoyed every bite. Then there's the woman who ordered her pizzas so well done that they practically had to be black. I was always the one to pull them out of the oven because everyone else was too afraid they'd burn them. Not her, though—she knew exactly how she liked it, and we were happy to deliver.

And oh, the couple we always joked with. Whenever I saw them coming and had a moment, I'd run to the door and pretend to lock it. We'd all share a laugh—those moments are what makes this job fun. And then there's the man who came in just about every day, always ordering a large Diet Coke and sitting at the same table. He wasn't just a regular customer; he became a true friend to the owner. They've gone on fishing and hunting trips together. It's incredible how something as simple as a daily routine can turn into a meaningful connection.

There are many more of these beloved, wonderful gifts to our lives than just the ones I mentioned, of course, but there are too many to count. You know who you are. You all are the reason I love coming to work. You make the craziness worth it, and you bring joy to my days. Thank you for being more than just customers. Thank you for being the bright spots in the madness.

So, as we wrap up this little journey through the madness that is the restaurant industry, I want to leave you with a final piece of advice. Ordering food doesn't have to be complicated. It doesn't have to be an ordeal. If you take one thing away from this book, let it be this: a little bit of consideration goes a long way. Whether you're ordering pizza, wings, or a cheesesteak, just remember that there's a real person on the other side of that transaction—someone who's juggling a million things at once and just trying to make sure you get your food as quickly as possible.

So, next time you place an order, take a moment to think about how you can make the process smoother for everyone involved. Know what you want before you call or step up to the counter. Don't add a bunch of items after the fact. Be polite. And for the love of all things cheesy, tip well.

And that, my friends, is the real secret to making your dining experience—and ours—a whole lot better. Happy ordering!

www.ingramcontent.com/pod-product-compliance
Lightning Source LLC
LaVergne TN
LVHW022000060526
838201LV00048B/1643